Designing Documents and Understanding Visuals

Supplement to Accompany
Handbooks by

Diana Hacker

Roger Munger
Boise State University, Idaho

Marcia F. Muth
University of Colorado at Denver

Karla Saari Kitalong
University of Central Florida

BEDFORD / ST. MARTIN'S   Boston ◆ New York

For information, write: Bedford/St. Martin's, 75 Arlington Street, Boston, MA 02116   (617-399-4000)

ISBN-10: 0-312-45266-7
ISBN-13: 978-0-312-45266-7

Acknowledgments

Page V–4: Page from "Nutrition Know How" from *Health* magazine. Copyright © 2004 by Hippocrates Partners. Reprinted with the permission of *Health.*

Page V–5 and Figure V7–4: Page and table from the *Journal of the American Medical Association.* Copyright © 2006 by American Medical Association. Reprinted with the permission of the *Journal of the American Medical Association.*

Figure V1–1: Screen shot of Boise State University Web site. Used by permission of Boise State University.

Figure V1–2: "Sprouting & Soaking Table" from Juliano Brotman, *Raw: The Uncook Book.* Copyright © 1999 by Juliano Brotman. Reprinted with the permission of HarperCollins Publishers.

Figures V1–3 and V2–6: Alaska Judicial Council staff, excerpts from "Appellate Evaluation of Judges Eligible for Reelection in 2006" (memorandum, April 24, 2006). Reprinted with the permission of the Alaska Judicial Council.

Figure V2–2: Default formatting for a word processor. Reprinted with the permission of Microsoft, Inc.

Figures V2–3 and V8–2: Pages from Tom Jehn and Jane Rosenzweig, *Writing in the Disciplines: Advice and Models.* Copyright © 2007 by Bedford/St. Martin's.

Figure V2–8: The National Zoological Park, Friends of the National Zoo, www.nationalzoo.si.edu. © 2007 Smithsonian Institution.

Figure V3–1: "Is Your Life Out of Control?" advertisement. Reprinted with the permission of the Art Institute of Boston/Lesley University.

Figure V3–2: "Installing Blade" safety instructions. Reprinted with the permission of WMH Tool Group, Inc.

Figure V3–8: Diana Hacker, *A Writer's Reference,* 6th edition. Copyright © 2007 by Bedford/St. Martin's.

Figure V3–12: "Lewis and Clark as Naturalists" Web site. Reprinted with the permission of the Smithsonian Institution, www.si.edu.

Figure V4–1: Diagram courtesy of King County, Washington, Wastewater Treatment Division.

Figure V4–2: Table and photograph from the Humane Society, *Guide to Vegetarian Eating.* Copyright © by The Humane Society of the United States. Reprinted with permission. Line Graph and Diagram courtesy of the United States Department of Agriculture. Pie Chart courtesy of the City of Santa Monica, California.

Figure V4–3: Table and figure. Copyright © 1998 by the American Medical Association. Reprinted with the permission of the *Journal of the American Medical Association.*

Figure V4–4: Modified from Ray et al., *Journal of Bone and Mineral Research* (January 1997): 24–35. Copyright © 1997. Reprinted courtesy of the United States Department of Health and Human Services.

Figure V6–2: Photograph: Bull rider. Reprinted with the permission of Professional Bull Riders, Inc.

Figure V6–4: Honda, "Green through and through." Reprinted with the permission of American Honda Motor Co., Inc.

Figure V7–1: "Spending Growth" chart. Reprinted with the permission of The Heritage Foundation.

Figures V7–2 and V7–3: Kodak Picture of the Day, October 22, 2000. Copyright © 2000 by Eastman Kodak Company. Reprinted with permission.

Figure V7–5: "Weather Helm" diagram. Courtesy of the American Sailing Association, www.asa.com.

Acknowledgments and copyrights are continued at the back of the book on page V-58, which constitutes an extension of the copyright page. It is a violation of the law to reproduce these selections by any means whatsoever without the written permission of the copyright holder.

V

Designing Documents and Understanding Visuals

V Designing Documents and Understanding Visuals

DESIGNING YOUR DOCUMENT

Whether the document you prepare is an essay, a research paper, a lab report, or a business letter, creating an effective design for it helps you achieve your purpose and meet the expectations of your readers. You may have noticed that you respond differently to documents depending on their appearance. For example, look quickly at the pages from two articles on pages V-4 and V-5. Which of the two articles seems more appealing to you?

If you prefer the article in *Health*, you're like many Americans — you like the look of a colorful, casual article and probably consider it friendly and easy to read. But if you were asked to choose which of the two articles seems more credible or trustworthy, you might say the article in the *Journal of the American Medical Association*. Its closely typed text, justified margins, dense table of data, and lack of color make it look more objective and scientific than the *Health* article.

As you can see, the same features that make the *Journal of the American Medical Association* seem more credible than *Health* might also make it less inviting to read. Like other scientific journals, however, the *Journal of the American Medical Association* freely uses headings, informative visuals, headers and footers, and other design features that help readers grasp the structure of the text at a glance and work their way through it.

Occasionally, college students create academic documents such as reports and research papers that look and read like a magazine or journal article. However, most of your college papers will not be as visually complex as the articles in the *Journal of the American Medical Association* and *Health*. Instead of calling for multiple columns, icons, and sidebars, your instructor will most likely expect to see double-spacing, one-inch margins, numbered pages, and indented block quotations — design options typical of academic documents.

V1

Making good design choices

The design choices you make will determine whether your document is readable and understandable for your intended audience. Using a word processing program, you can easily create a three-column layout, add color headings, use several fonts, and insert clip art. However, these design choices might not be appropriate for your

PAGE FROM *HEALTH* MAGAZINE

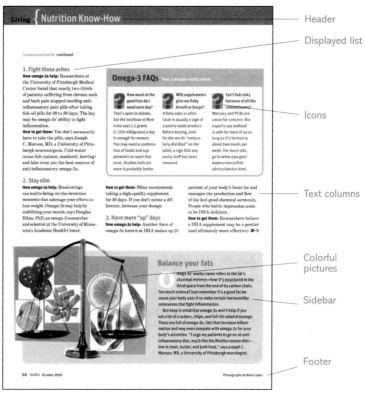

Header

Displayed list

Icons

Text columns

Colorful pictures

Sidebar

Footer

Pages from articles in two magazines
Which article looks more inviting, the one from *Health* magazine (above) or the one from the *Journal of the American Medical Association* (facing page)? Which looks more credible?
(*Source: Health* magazine)

writing situation. Focusing on the four goals of effective design presented in this section will help you make good design choices to achieve your purpose and meet the expectations of your readers both in and outside of the classroom. Remember, however, that good document design cannot save a poorly written or organized document. (See the writing process chapters in your handbook.)

V1-a Achieve your purpose.

Like most writers, you usually have a purpose for creating a document. College essays often need to convey a particular theme, argument,

PAGE FROM *JOURNAL OF THE AMERICAN MEDICAL ASSOCIATION* — Header

— Justified margins

— Text columns

— Data table

— Footer

LOW-FAT DIETARY PATTERN AND RISK OF CARDIOVASCULAR DISEASE

Follow-up

At trial conclusion, 2404 women (4.9%) were deceased, 1553 (3.2%) had stopped follow-up, and 527 (1.1%) were lost to follow-up. Five percent (4.7%) of women in the intervention and 4.0% in the comparison group withdrew, were considered lost to follow-up, or had stopped providing outcomes information for longer than 18 months (Figure 1). Eleven percent (11.4%) of women had terminated the intervention, as defined by neither attending group sessions nor providing self-monitoring information through phone or individual visits for 18 months.

CVD Risk Factors

At year 3, women in the intervention group compared with those in the comparison group showed small but significant decreases in body weight,[39] waist circumference,[39] diastolic blood pressure, LDL-C level (3.55 mg/dL [0.09 mmol/L]), and factor VIIc level (Table 2). The dietary intervention had no statistically significant effects on levels of triglycerides or HDL-C; ratio of total cholesterol to HDL-C; levels of non–HDL-C, lipoprotein(a), glucose, or insulin; or insulin resistance as estimated by homeostasis model assessment[36]; in the latter 3 factors, there were trends toward improvement. The observed absolute LDL-C change of 2.7 mg/dL (0.07 mmol/L) after 6 years was similar to the 2.3-mg/dL (0.06-mmol/L) change predicted using current equations based on differences in fatty acid intakes.[37] Carotenoid levels, a reflection of increased vegetable consumption, were significantly higher.

CVD Outcomes

After a mean of 8.1 years of follow-up, the observed incidence rate for major CHD (MI/CHD death, 3.6 per 1000 person-years) in the comparison group was 30% lower than projected in the design. No significant effects of the dietary intervention were observed for major CHD (HR, 0.98, 95% CI, 0.88-1.09) or composite CHD (CHD/revascularization; HR, 0.97; 95% CI, 0.90-1.06) vs the comparison group (TABLE 4). The incidences of total, fatal, or nonfatal stroke were not influenced by the dietary intervention (HR, 1.02; 95% CI, 0.90-1.15), nor was a composite measure of CVD (CHD/revascularization/stroke; HR, 0.98; 95% CI, 0.92-1.05). The monitoring plan for the Dietary Modification Trial specified 2 primary outcomes (breast and colorectal cancer) and 2 secondary outcomes (major CHD and death from other causes). The 95% CI for major CHD, adjusted for these 4 outcomes using a Bonferroni correction,

Table 3. Baseline and Follow-up Nutrient Intakes*

	Baseline, Mean (SD)		Year 1, Mean (SD)			Year 6, Mean (SD)		
	Intervention	Comparison	Intervention	Comparison	Difference Mean (95% CI)	Intervention	Comparison	Difference Mean (95% CI)
Total energy, kcal/d	1790.2 (710.1)	1789.4 (703.0)	1600.5 (644.2)	1593.8 (644.0)	-93.4 (-104.8 to -81.9)	1431.8 (561.7)	1646.2 (639.5)	-114.3 (-126.8 to -101.8)
Daily intakes, % of energy								
Total fat	37.8 (6.1)	37.8 (6.0)	24.3 (7.5)	36.1 (6.9)	-10.7 (-10.9 to -10.6)	28.8 (6.4)	37.0 (7.3)	-6.2 (-6.3 to -6.0)
Saturated fat	12.7 (2.5)	12.7 (2.5)	8.1 (2.6)	11.8 (2.9)	-3.7 (-3.7 to -3.6)	9.5 (3.2)	12.4 (3.1)	-2.9 (-3.0 to -2.8)
Monounsaturated fat	14.4 (2.3)	14.4 (2.3)	8.9 (3.1)	13.3 (2.9)	-4.4 (-4.5 to -4.4)	10.8 (3.5)	14.2 (3.1)	-3.3 (-3.4 to -3.3)
Polyunsaturated fat	7.8 (2.0)	7.8 (2.0)	5.2 (1.8)	7.2 (2.1)	-2.0 (-2.0 to -2.0)	6.1 (2.1)	7.5 (2.1)	-1.5 (-1.5 to -1.4)
Total trans fatty acid	2.7 (1.1)	2.8 (1.1)	1.8 (0.8)	2.5 (1.1)	-0.6 (-0.9 to -0.8)	1.8 (0.9)	2.4 (1.1)	-0.6 (-0.6 to -0.6)
Protein	16.5 (3.0)	16.4 (3.0)	17.7 (3.1)	16.9 (3.2)	0.8 (0.8 to 0.9)	17.7 (3.4)	17.1 (3.3)	0.6 (0.5 to 0.6)
Carbohydrate	45.6 (6.3)	45.6 (6.2)	58.3 (8.9)	46.0 (8.0)	10.3 (10.2 to 10.5)	53.9 (9.8)	45.9 (8.8)	6.1 (7.9 to 6.3)
Dietary fiber, g/d	15.4 (6.4)	15.4 (6.4)	18.1 (7.5)	14.9 (6.5)	3.2 (3.0 to 3.3)	16.9 (7.5)	14.4 (6.4)	2.4 (2.3 to 2.6)
Soluble fiber, g/d	4.2 (1.7)	4.2 (1.8)	4.9 (2.0)	4.0 (1.8)	0.8 (0.8 to 0.9)	4.5 (2.0)	3.8 (1.7)	0.6 (0.6 to 0.7)
Dietary folate equivalent, μg/d	269.2 (136.6)	269.3 (138.1)	398.5 (216.0)	346.1 (195.1)	52.4 (48.8 to 66.2)	469.1 (206.8)	422.5 (180.0)	46.6 (42.5 to 50.6)
Cholesterol, mg/d	260.5 (139.0)	260.0 (135.8)	172.4 (99.3)	229.8 (128.7)	-57.5 (-59.7 to -55.3)	193.8 (118.7)	243.5 (143.2)	-49.9 (-52.7 to -47.2)
Intakes, servings/d								
Vegetables and fruits	3.6 (1.8)	3.6 (1.8)	5.1 (2.3)	3.9 (2.0)	1.2 (1.2 to 1.2)	4.9 (2.4)	3.8 (2.0)	1.1 (1.1 to 1.2)
Grains	4.7 (2.5)	4.8 (2.5)	5.1 (2.7)	4.2 (2.3)	0.8 (0.8 to 0.9)	4.3 (2.4)	3.8 (2.2)	0.5 (0.4 to 0.5)
Whole grains	1.1 (0.8)	1.1 (0.8)	1.4 (0.9)	1.1 (0.7)	0.3 (0.3 to 0.3)	1.2 (0.9)	1.0 (0.7)	0.2 (0.2 to 0.2)
Intakes, servings/wk								
Beef	0.1 (0.7)	0.1 (0.7)	0.2 (0.8)	0.2 (0.7)	0.0 (0.0 to 0.0)	0.3 (1.0)	0.2 (0.9)	0.0 (0.0 to 0.1)
Nuts	1.2 (1.7)	1.5 (2.3)	1.6 (1.1)	1.3 (1.9)	-0.8 (-0.9 to -0.7)	1.9 (2.5)	1.5 (2.5)	-0.8 (-0.9 to -0.8)
Fish	1.9 (1.6)	1.9 (1.7)	1.9 (1.7)	1.8 (1.7)	0.1 (0.0 to 0.1)	2.0 (1.7)	2.0 (1.9)	0.0 (-0.1 to 0.0)

Abbreviations: CI, confidence interval; P/S, ratio of polyunsaturated fat to saturated fat.
*Nutrient intakes were available on 19470 and 29216 participants at baseline, and 18058 and 26743 at year 1 and 14866 and 22958 at year 6 in the intervention and comparison groups, respectively. Data on servings of types of food was available on 19470 and 29216 participants at baseline, 18067 and 26743 at year 1, and 14774 and 22713 at year 6 in the intervention and comparison groups respectively.
†All differences significant at P<.001 from a 2-sample test except for soy at year 3 (P = .02), and fish at year 6 (P = .40).
‡No soy intake was reported by 87.0%, 84.9%, and 90.1% of participants at baseline, year 1, and year 6, respectively.

(*Source:* American Medical Association)

or point of view. In business, you might want to present a proposal, explain how to carry out a task, propose a budget, or present a market analysis. Your challenge is to take your readers' needs and your purpose into account as you make design choices. Making choices that achieve your purposes will increase your credibility as a writer.

If your purpose is to persuade a prospective employer to contact you for an interview, you will likely choose design elements for your cover letter that reflect established business conventions (see the business writing section in your handbook). If your purpose is to help your readers complete a task, you might choose to include numbered steps (see Figure V1–1).

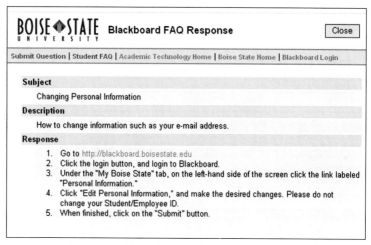

FIGURE V1-1 **Web page with numbered list**
A numbered list offers step-by-step instructions to help readers complete a task.
(*Source:* Boise State University)

V1-b Help your readers.

Whether you are writing an essay for a class or preparing a business document, identifying your readers is an important step in creating an effective design. For most college papers, your primary reader is your instructor, and your secondary readers are your peers or others. In business, you might be asked to address a specific group, such as farmers or computer programmers or consumers of your products.

In deciding how to design your document, consider ways to attract your readers' attention to the most important points and guide them through the document. You might consider whether your readers are likely to read every word of your document or to skim it for key points. Perhaps visuals, such as tables, graphs, or diagrams, would make information more accessible (see Figure V1–2).

You might also consider how your readers will use your document. If your instructor needs extra space for writing comments on your draft, use wide margins and double-spaced text. If you write an e-mail, use short paragraphs and skip lines between paragraphs to make the message easy to read on a computer screen. Thinking about such issues as you make your design choices means you'll have a better chance of reaching your readers.

Sprouting & Soaking Table		
	SOAKING TIME HOURS	SPROUTING TIME DAYS
Almonds	8	No sprouting
Barley	6	2
Buckwheat	6	2
Chickpeas (a.k.a.: Garbanzo Beans)	8	2–3
Flax Seeds	$^1/_2$	No sprouting
Kamut	7	2–3
Lentil Beans	7	3
Oat Groats	6	2
Quinoa	2	1
Rye	8	3
Sesame Seeds	6	2
Spelt	7	2
Walnuts	4	No sprouting
Wheat berries	7	2–3
Wild rice	9	3–5
All other nuts	6	No sprouting

FIGURE V1-2 **Table from a gardening handbook**
A table presents information concisely and helps readers grasp the information quickly. (*Source:* Juliano Brotman, 1999)

V1-c Meet format expectations.

Readers, including your instructor and your peers, have expectations about how different types of documents should look. Usually your readers expect your academic documents to be typed on a computer, double-spaced, with headers and numbered pages. Your instructor will probably want you to include a cover page with your name, the title of your paper, the course number and section, the date, and perhaps other information. Your instructor might also have expectations about appropriate visual evidence, such as graphs, tables, photographs, or other illustrations, depending on the field and the assignment. Many college courses follow the formatting guidelines of the Modern Language Association (MLA), the American Psychological Association (APA), or *The Chicago Manual of Style* (CMS). (See the appropriate documentation section in your handbook for advice on formatting an academic document.) Check your course syllabus to see whether your instructor requires a specific format.

Readers also have format expectations for different types of business documents. Prospective employers expect your résumé to present your qualifications in clear categories with descriptive headings such as *Experience* and *Education*. Some organizations prefer that memos

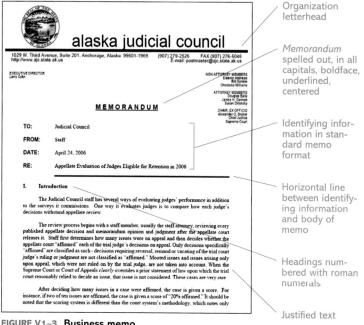

FIGURE V1-3 **Business memo**
Organizations typically expect memos to be formatted in a standard way and often provide a template with the required elements in place. (*Source:* Alaska Judicial Council)

use a standard format. Before formatting a business document, determine the expectations of the organization you are writing for or find an effective example of the type of document you intend to write and study its design features. See Figure V1–3 for a sample business memo.

TIP: Create a template with your word processing software for types of documents you create frequently, such as memos, letters, and reports.

V1-d Use visuals to convey information concisely.

Some documents might benefit from the addition of graphs, diagrams, maps, photographs, or other visuals that convey information concisely and reinforce your written text (see Figure V1–4). You might create visuals yourself or use visuals from other sources, giving credit and requesting permission if needed (see "avoiding plagiarism" in your handbook). Keep in mind, however, that your visuals should be appropriate for your purpose and your readers, not used merely as decoration (see Figure V1–5).

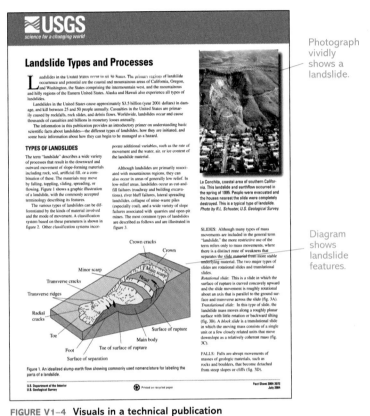

Photograph vividly shows a landslide.

Diagram shows landslide features.

FIGURE V1–4 **Visuals in a technical publication**
Visuals can convey information succinctly and clearly. (*Source:* US Geological Survey)

TIP: Check your spreadsheet software for tools to help you create visuals such as charts and graphs. Check your word processing software for tools to help you create and format tables.

V2

Helping readers find information

Readers usually have a specific reason for reading your writing. Your instructor might read your paper to evaluate your understanding of a topic or to find out your views on an issue. Often people read

FIGURE V1–5 Ineffective use of a visual
Clip art often does not convey information or serve a useful purpose. Here it is a distraction from the main point of a technical PowerPoint presentation. (*Source:* NASA)

a document to learn the answer to a specific question or to learn how to complete a task. Depending on a person's reason for reading, he or she might read a document from start to finish, skip around, skim it, or read only specific sections. Your goal in designing your document is to use design features that help readers quickly find the information they need.

V2-a Use headings to guide readers.

Readers of documents look for cues about what is most important and about how various sections are related to one another. Headings can provide such cues. Clear headings guide your readers by showing a document's organization. Though headings are often unnecessary in short documents, they can focus the attention of readers while providing a useful pathway through complex documents such as research papers, lab reports, business proposals, and Web documents. (For more details, see "headings" in your handbook.)

Use fonts in different styles and sizes to distinguish between levels of headings (see Figure V2–1). Using consistent formatting tell those reading the utility brochure that they can and should take a few simple energy-saving steps to do their part for the environment. To support their views, energy-efficiency advocates draw on a traditional set of beliefs as to what is technically effective, and to some extent what is psychologically effective.

First-level heading

Our Collection of Myths

For the past few years we have been collecting myths about energy and buildings, a list that quickly expanded from a few personal favorites to several dozen examples, as friends and colleagues have been eager to share their myths (Diamond 1998). We have chosen to organize this list of myths about people, energy, and buildings into four categories, based on who is telling the myths to whom: 1) Myths told to consumers by utilities, public institutions and non-profits; 2) Myths consumers tell themselves; 3) Myths told by design professionals (architects and engineers) to clients; and 4) Myths told by energy professionals to consumers and each other. By organizing the myths based on which group of people tells them, we can start to look for patterns or motives for why these myths develop and continue. How do these myths influence our policies and efforts to promote energy conservation? Does recognizing that different groups tell different stories help in crafting public policy? Does revealing the truth or lack of truth in these myths further our understanding? Our hope is that by studying these myths we can understand how we construct policy that ultimately affects the way we design and inhabit buildings.

Second-level heading

Myths Told to Consumers by Utilities, Public Institutions, Non-Profits

We give two examples here of myths that have appeared in countless guides and brochures provided by utilities, governments and energy conservation advocates. These myths are often in the form of "ten simple things you can do to save the earth/planet/environment" and are typically directed to homeowners and renters. The information from these guides often cannot be traced to any authoritative source, but are commonly borrowed from similar, earlier documents, having gained a relatively unquestioned claim to truth simply by tradition. These tips are usually offered as generalizations, and without quantification. If real savings do result, in most cases they would be too small to be noticed at the consumer level, even if in aggregate—from the utility or national level—they result in observable savings. These recommendations provide positive actions that a homeowner can take immediately, hence their appeal to recommendation-givers. Some might argue that by taking a small positive step in the right direction it will be easier to have the homeowner undertake larger actions, even if the true energy savings from this small step alone is inconsequential. On the other hand, if homeowners do not see results from their actions, they may be less likely to bother with further energy-efficiency recommendations.

Third-level heading

Myth #1. Cleaning the refrigerator coils improves refrigerator efficiency. There is some intuitive logic that if you clean the years of accumulated dust from the surfaces of the coils, the heat transfer will improve. Unfortunately, there is little data to support this claim when it comes to refrigerator coils. A review of measured tests with refrigerators showed that there was no or little evidence of improved efficiency from cleaning the coils

FIGURE V2–1 **Report with three levels of headings**
Headings in a report should be visually distinct (also see Figure V2–2).
(*Source:* Lawrence Berkeley National Laboratory)

for each level of heading makes your text easier to read and easier to use, whether your reader is scrutinizing every word or scanning only key points. Unless your instructor asks you to use a particular style, such as APA or MLA, create your own formatting style so that your heading levels differ from each other and from the main text.

TIP: Use the styles and formatting feature of your word processing program to consistently apply your design choices to headings and other page elements (see Figure V2–2). If you decide later to change

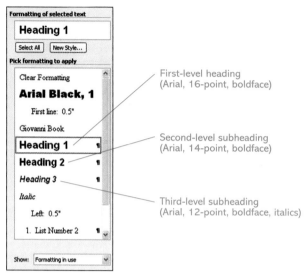

First-level heading
(Arial, 16-point, boldface)

Second-level subheading
(Arial, 14-point, boldface)

Third-level subheading
(Arial, 12-point, boldface, italics)

FIGURE V2–2 Default formatting for three levels of headings in a word processor (*Source:* Microsoft Word XP)

the style of any element, you can make the change once and the word processor automatically updates all those elements in the document.

Headings should be as brief and as informative as possible. Headings on the same level of organization should be written in parallel structure — all *-ing* phrases, all noun phrases, or all questions, for instance. Headings also should be consistently aligned. Although some academic style guides specify centered headings (see Figure V2–3), left alignment is stronger from a design perspective (see Figure V2–4). If you are writing a paper for a course, check with your instructor about how to format headings.

Web pages tend to have more headings than other types of documents because they are designed to help readers find information quickly on a computer screen. If you are designing a Web page, consider what readers might want to find on your site, and clearly connect your headings and content to readers' needs. For example, a Web site designed to attract runners for a road race might include the headings Registration, Race Route, Training, and Sponsors.

For longer documents such as reports, a table of contents is a useful aid for readers (see Figure V2–5). The table of contents should include the same headings and subheadings as the document as well

ALL and HTN in One Client 1 —— Page
header

Historical and Physical Assessment

Physical History First-level
heading
E.B. is a 16-year-old white male 179 cm tall weighing 86.9 kg.
He was admitted to the hospital on April 14, 2006, due to decreased Second-
level
platelets and a need for a PRBC transfusion. He was diagnosed in heading
October 2005 with T-cell acute lymphoblastic leukemia (ALL), after a
2-week period of decreased energy, decreased oral intake, easy
bruising, and petechia. The client had experienced a 20-lb weight
loss in the previous 6 months. At the time of diagnosis, his CBC
showed a WBC count of 32, an H & H of 13/38, and a platelet count
of 34,000. His initial chest X-ray showed an anterior mediastinal
mass. Echocardiogram showed a structurally normal heart. He began
induction chemotherapy on October 12, 2005, receiving vincristine,
6-mercaptopurine, doxorubicin, intrathecal methotrexate, and then
high-dose methotrexate per protocol. During his hospital stay he
required packed red cells and platelets on two different occasions.
He was diagnosed with hypertension (HTN) due to systolic blood
pressure readings consistently ranging between 130s and 150s and
was started on nifedipine. E.B. has a history of mild ADHD,
migraines, and deep vein thrombosis (DVT). He has tolerated the
induction and consolidation phases of chemotherapy well and is now
in the maintenance phase, in which he receives a daily dose of
mercaptopurine, weekly doses of methotrexate, and intermittent
doses of steroids.

Psychosocial History

There is a possibility of a depressive episode a year previously

FIGURE V2–3 **Academic paper with centered headings**
Some academic style guides, such as MLA, APA, and *Chicago* (CMS),
recommend centered headings for at least the first level. This page from
an APA-style paper uses centered headings for the first level and flush
left italic headings for the second level. (*Source:* Tom Jehn and Jane Rosenzweig, *Writing in the Disciplines: Advice and Models*)

as page numbers for each heading. Readers thus can understand the
organization of the document at a glance and can quickly find the
information they want.

TIP: Word processors can create a table of contents automatically. If
you revise your document, the word processor automatically updates the table of contents.

applicant, it does not matter whether you prefer these tests or not. These tests are gaining in popularity, and job seekers should expect to take some type of employment test. Mizell explains, "Although an applicant has the right to refuse them, it's not illegal for an employer to ask for any test, even something as obscure and unproven as numerology" [16]. Although applicants cannot "prepare" for some of these tests such as personality tests, the best course of action is to answer them honestly. Second guessing a personality test is very difficult, and some of the more sophisticated ones have built-in mechanisms for catching applicants in a lie. For skills-based tests, technical communicators can prepare by reviewing core knowledge and skills essential to performing the job.

Online Mistakes

Just as the Internet has made hiring more complicated for employers, so too has it made the job hunt more complicated for technical communicators. The Internet's global reach, size, speed, and lack of privacy controls often lure technical communicators into making mistakes that will at best cause them to waste their time and money and at worst result in their getting fired or having their identities stolen. The following are the most common mistakes technical communicators can make while searching for a job online, including advice on how to avoid these mistakes.

Searching for a Job Using Your Current Employer's Resources

Recruiters frequently comment on how surprised they are at the numbers of applicants obviously using their current employer's e-mail, phone, and time to search for another job. If applicants are searching for another job while on company time, recruiters assume they are not productively working. Moreover, if applicants feel free to waste their current employer's resources, recruiters worry what else they might feel free to do.

ADVICE: Search for a job on your own time. Avoid using company resources by getting a personal e-mail account (many Internet sites offer free e-mail services). Do not be tempted to use your employer's printer, phone lines, mail supplies, or fax. Doing so may result in you losing your job (and possibly a good reference).

Failing to Protect Your Privacy

Résumé theft is a growing business for identity thieves. Take a look at your résumé and ask yourself what an identity thief may be interested in: your name, phone number, e-mail address, postal address, detailed employment history, etc. Eager to find employment, job applicants provide identity thieves with an electronic treasure chest of data when they post materials to web-based databases. The threat of identity theft and a more general unease with posting confidential material on the Internet are causing many applicants to rethink their online job-search strategies. For example, a recent article in *Workforce* reported, "Nearly 70 percent of executives' companies post jobs on the Internet. However, 65 percent of the execs said that they wouldn't post their own résumés online, or that they had serious qualms about doing so" [24]. Both job boards and job seekers are guilty of practices that fail to protect confidential data.

Some job boards do not adequately disclose what they do with your résumés, contact information, and other personal data once you post it to the site. A site may share your data with other companies without your

FIGURE V2–4 Report with left-aligned headings
Headings aligned at the left margin create a strong visual element down the left side of the page.

V2-b Repeat design elements to guide readers.

Consistently placing and formatting headings is one form of effective repetition. Another simple design strategy is the use of repeated headers and footers. A *running header* is a line of information that

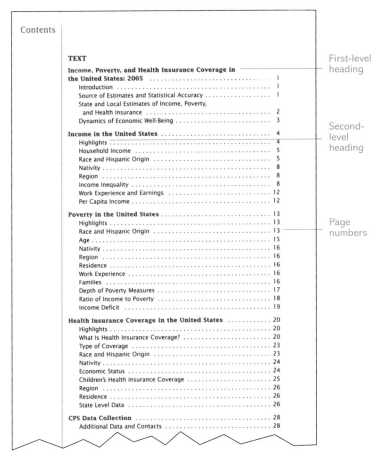

Contents

First-level
heading

Second-
level
heading

Page
numbers

FIGURE V2–5 **Table of contents for a report**
The table of contents shows the organization of the report at a glance.
The two levels of headings are visually distinguished by color, font size,
and font type. (*Source:* US Census Bureau)

appears consistently at the top of each page of your document (see
Figure V2–6); a *running footer* appears consistently at the bottom
of each page (see Figure V2–7). Within the header or the footer
writers sometimes include information such as the document title,
the filename, the date, the page number, or a graphic.

TIP: Once you create a header or footer, your word processor can
automatically insert it on each page.

Appellate Review Memo
April 24, 2006
Page 2

---

whether the case was affirmed, partly affirmed, reversed, remanded, vacated, or dismissed. Also, the court system tends to attribute the appeal to the last judge of record rather than determine which

---

FIGURE V2–6 Sample document header
This header is from page 2 of the business memo in Figure V1–3. It includes an abbreviated subject, the date, and the page number. A horizontal line separates the header from the body of the memo. (*Source:* Alaska Judicial Council)

■ **Use a home soil kit** to check the pH level of your garden. Do so once a year. Have the pH level of your garden professionally analyzed once every three years.

can add organic matter such as compost to improve soil drainage. Proper drainage is one of the most important elements of a healthy garden.

GARDENER'S TOOLBOX
Page 2

FIGURE V2–7 Sample footer from a newsletter
Footers may include the filename, the page number, the date, and other elements such as a graphic, as in this footer.

Web sites often include a consistently placed logo, usually in the upper left corner, on each page. Repetition of a logo helps readers quickly determine where they are and when they have left the Web site for another site. Many Web sites also include a set of consistent navigation links on every page. These show readers what is available on the site and help them move around the site. Figure V2–8 illustrates both types of repetition on a Web site.

V3

Emphasizing important information

Many readers do not have enough time or, in some cases, motivation to read your entire document from start to finish. Even your instructor might not read your essay word-for-word. Instead, readers want to find specific information quickly. Some readers might want to focus only on your main points, skimming some of your supporting

Repetition of logos

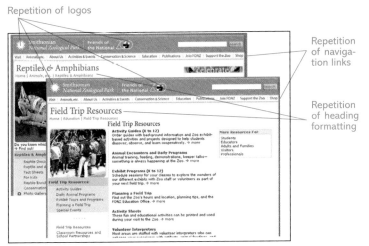

Repetition of navigation links

Repetition of heading formatting

FIGURE V2–8 Use of repetition on a Web site (*Source:* Smithsonian Institution, National Zoological Park)

details. To accommodate all your readers' needs, be sure to use document design features that call attention to important information.

V3-a Make important information clearly visible.

If you want readers to find, read, and remember information that you consider important, format your document so that such information stands out. As you begin work on a document, ask "What is the main message I want to get across?" Once you have decided on that message, think of ways to emphasize it. For example, if you are designing a brochure or a flyer, you might want to use one large headline surrounded by a significant amount of space, as the designer of the brochure did in Figure V3–1. If you are designing instructions, you will want to place safety information in a location where readers will see it first (see Figure V3–2).

V3-b Use fonts to call attention to different kinds of text.

Word processing software allows you to change fonts, or typefaces, to increase readability, add emphasis, or set a particular tone in your writing. Such choices can make your document clearer and more attractive, but inappropriate or excessive use of fonts can

Do you want to stop smoking?

Are you experiencing sickness, shortness of breath
or other medical problems related to smoking?

Have you given up other things in your life
to buy cigarettes?

Have others complained about your smoking?

Are you depressed?

Have you felt hopeless for a month or more?

Do you wake up at night without getting back
to sleep for more than two days a week?

Have you felt like hurting yourself or others?

Are you in an unsafe relationship?

Has your partner hit, slapped, kicked, punched
or hurt you in any way?

Are you repeatedly called names, told you are
worthless, verbally threatened or made to feel afraid?

Do you feel safe in your home?

Are you being forced to have sex or are you
having sex without protection?

Do you have problems with
alcohol or drugs?

Are you drinking or using drugs to start the day?

Do you try to hide your drinking or drug use?

Do you feel guilt or feel the need to control your use?

Are others annoyed or affected by your behavior?

FIGURE V3–1 Brochure design emphasizing important information
The faint words on the left panel, the brochure cover, serve as a suggestive background, but the image immediately draws the eye and the pattern of light guides readers to the central question: "Is your life out of control?" The headings — all questions — are parallel in form. They also are larger than the text, for emphasis, and are separated by white space so the questions stand out and readers clearly see the main topics. (*Source:* Art Institute of Boston/Lesley University)

clutter your work. Although most college papers use a conventional font in a 12-point size, not all 12-point fonts appear the same size, nor do all fonts convey the same tone. For most college and professional writing, unusual fonts are inappropriate and can suggest a lack of seriousness (see Figure V3–3).

Fonts are generally classified in two categories: *serif* and *sans serif*. Serif fonts, such as Times New Roman and Courier New, have small tails, or serifs, at the ends of the letters. Sans serif ("without

---

Installing Blade

NOTE: The blade must be mounted first before rails can be adjusted.

To install or replace a blade, proceed as follows:

⚠CAUTION Use care when working with or around sharp saw blade.

1. Disconnect machine from power source.

2. Remove table insert, then remove arbor nut and collar.

3. Install blade, making sure the cutting teeth at the top of the blade point toward the front of the saw.

4. Slide the collar on to the arbor and start the arbor nut on the threads. (NOTE: Right-hand threads; turn clockwise to tighten.) Snug the arbor nut against the collar and blade with the provided arbor wrench, while holding blade with thumb and finger tips.

5. Wedge a block of wood between the blade and table to prevent blade rotation, then tighten the arbor nut securely with the arbor wrench. See Figure 6.

FIGURE V3-2 **Instructions in a manual for a table saw**
The safety information is prominently displayed and is placed first, to be read before the user would begin following the numbered steps. The word *CAUTION* conveys the seriousness of the hazard, and the boldface words identify the source of the hazard: a sharp saw blade.
(*Source:* WMH Tool Group)

serif") fonts, such as Arial and Helvetica, have solid, straight lines and no tails at the tips of the letters. Sans serif fonts have a clean look, but they are less readable than serif fonts, especially in long passages. Typically, serif fonts are used for text in the body of a document and sans serif fonts are used for headings and titles. Using only one of each type in your document will give your design an uncluttered look and provide the maximum readability and emphasis.

Font styles, such as italics and boldface, can also provide emphasis. When you *italicize* a word or a passage, you call readers' attention to it. Italics is used in certain situations (for more details, see the mechanics section in your handbook):

- For book, film, or software titles: *Wuthering Heights*, *Apocalypse Now*.

- For foreign words: My Lithuanian grandmother makes my favorite dish, *kugelis* ("potato cake").

- For words mentioned as themselves: We overused the word *navigate* in our user manual.

In technical and business writing, terms are sometimes italicized at their first mention in a document or a chapter: "AIDS patients monitor their levels of *helper T-cells* because these cells detect antigens in the body and activate other cells to fight the antigens."

Use italics for emphasis, not for large blocks of text. Italicized words appear lighter in weight than nonitalicized words. This lightness, coupled with the slant of the letters, makes italics unsuitable for sustained reading.

Times New Roman	An estimated 40 percent of young children have an imaginary friend.
Courier New	An estimated 40 percent of young children have an imaginary friend.
Arial	An estimated 40 percent of young children have an imaginary friend.
Curlz MT	An estimated 40 percent of young children have an imaginary friend.

FIGURE V3–3 Four different fonts in the same size, for comparison

Some fonts are more suitable than others for business and academic documents. Times New Roman, for instance, takes up less space than most other fonts and is highly readable. A decorative font like Curlz MT would set an inappropriate tone in all but the most casual documents.

Roberta Gann

1234 West Gem Street
Boise, ID 83704

208-555-7617
rlgann@hotmail.com

Professional Profile

Versatile professional with expertise in communicating **technical concepts** and graduate training in **mathematics** and **computer programming**. Solid background in **statistics**, **learning new technology**, and **producing print** and **online materials**. Adaptable and effective in **high-demand**, **constantly-changing environments**. Proven record in addressing **customer** and **user needs** with excellent **interpersonal**, **communication**, and **organizational** skills.

Education

M.A.   **Mathematics Education**, State University of New York at Albany, December 1996.

B.A.   **Mathematics**, State University of New York at Albany, Academic Excellence in Mathematics Award, May 1995.

FIGURE V3–4 Overuse of boldface text in a résumé

With so many words emphasized in the Professional Profile section, readers might stop paying attention to the text entirely.

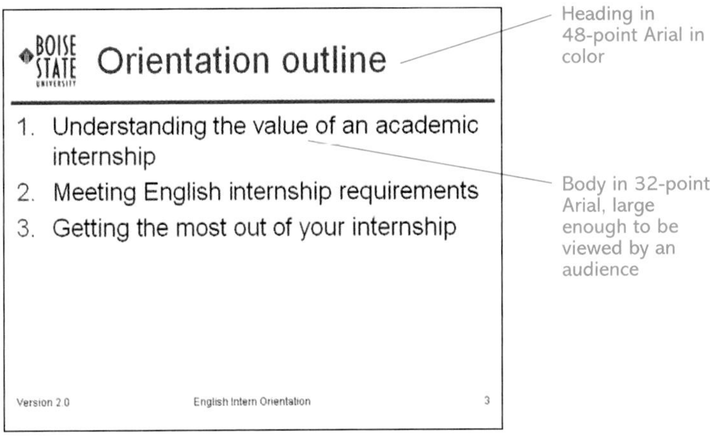

FIGURE V3–5 **Presentation slide with effective use of fonts**
Varying font sizes and colors is an effective technique for a visual that will be viewed by an audience at some distance.

Boldface style is suitable for emphasis only. Too much boldface dilutes the impact of what you want to emphasize and makes your document difficult to read (see Figure V3–4). In academic and business writing, your readers expect you to choose emphatic words, not to rely on boldface for emphasis. In general, reserve boldface primarily for headings.

Using too many fonts, font sizes, and font styles in one document is distracting to your readers. However, in some instances using a different font is an effective design strategy. Your headings will stand out from the rest of your text when you use a different font and font style (see V1-b). Sometimes you may need to use a larger size for signs, posters, and visuals for oral presentations (such as PowerPoint slides). In such cases, check if your text is easy to read by standing back from your document at the distance of your intended readers (see Figure V3–5).

V3-c Use displayed lists to highlight information or present a sequence.

Lists are easier to read when they are displayed rather than run into your text. In either case, a list should be introduced with an independent clause followed by a colon. (See "lists" in your handbook.)

LIST RUN INTO TEXT

Movies are rated by the film-rating board of the Classification and Rating Administration (CARA) based on several criteria, including the following: overall theme, language use, presence of violence, presence of nudity and sexual content, and combined use of these elements in one film.

DISPLAYED LIST

Movies are rated by the film-rating board of the Classification and Rating Administration (CARA) based on several criteria, including the following:

- overall theme
- language use
- presence of violence
- presence of nudity and sexual content
- combined use of these elements in one film

One type of displayed list uses a mark called a bullet to set off information, as in the preceding list. Use a bulleted list to indicate main points, reasons, or items when the order isn't significant (see Figure V3–6).

A numbered list can indicate ranking or emphasize sequence, especially in instructional writing (see Figure V3–7).

TIP: Use your word processor's bullets and numbering feature to consistently apply formatting to your lists.

Removable Labels

Labels and stickers to be removed from a backing or liner on letter mail and reused (such as "sandwich labels") must meet the following guidelines:

- When applied to a stainless steel surface, the adhesive on the backing or liner, which is permanently attached to the mailpiece, must have a minimum peel-adhesion value of 8 ounces per inch.

- When applied to the face of the backing or liner, the adhesive on the removable label must have a minimum peel-adhesion value of 2 ounces per inch.

- When reapplied to a stainless steel surface, the adhesive on the removable label must have a minimum peel-adhesion value of 8 ounces per inch.

FIGURE V3–6 **Bulleted list in a manual**
Bullets are used because the order of the guidelines is not important. Note that the list is introduced by an independent clause followed by a colon and that the list items are in parallel structure. (*Source:* US Postal Service)

Top Five Qualities or Skills Employers Seek

According to a 2005 survey by the National Association of Colleges and Employers, employers want to hire people with the following qualities or skills:

1. Communication skills
2. Honesty/integrity
3. Interpersonal skills
4. Strong work ethic
5. Teamwork skills

FIGURE V3-7 **Numbered list showing ranked items**
The numbered list presents the items according to the ranking they received in the survey. A numbered list is also useful for presenting steps in a sequence.

V3-d Use white space to frame important information.

White space (also referred to as *negative space*) is the area within a document that is free of text or visuals. Areas of white space give the eye a rest and can frame important information. As a design device, white space allows you to emphasize titles, headings, labels, and other elements of your document.

White space makes an important contribution to the appearance of your documents. If you have written college papers, you have probably used white space to assist your readers. For example, one-inch margins and double-spacing provide a break for readers' eyes. Closely spaced lines without much white space interfere with readers' ability to keep their place in the text and make a document seem uninviting. When you indent the first line of each paragraph, the space helps the reader identify a new paragraph. Indenting a long quotation ("block" quotation) sets it off and marks it as a special kind of text (see Figure V3–8; also see "indenting long quotations" in your handbook).

If you simply separate sections of your paper by hitting the enter key an extra time or two, you will add too much white space between sections. Too much extra space might break your readers' attention and make it difficult to follow your points.

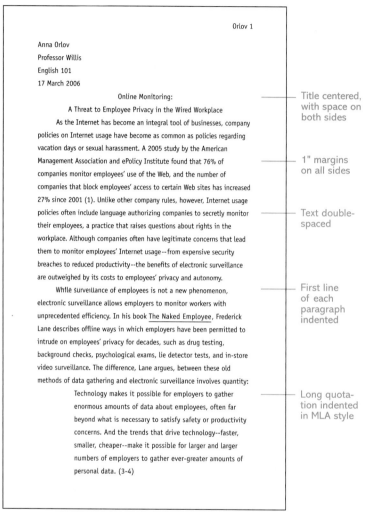

Orlov 1

Anna Orlov

Professor Willis

English 101

17 March 2006

Online Monitoring:

A Threat to Employee Privacy in the Wired Workplace

As the Internet has become an integral tool of businesses, company policies on Internet usage have become as common as policies regarding vacation days or sexual harassment. A 2005 study by the American Management Association and ePolicy Institute found that 76% of companies monitor employees' use of the Web, and the number of companies that block employees' access to certain Web sites has increased 27% since 2001 (1). Unlike other company rules, however, Internet usage policies often include language authorizing companies to secretly monitor their employees, a practice that raises questions about rights in the workplace. Although companies often have legitimate concerns that lead them to monitor employees' Internet usage--from expensive security breaches to reduced productivity--the benefits of electronic surveillance are outweighed by its costs to employees' privacy and autonomy.

While surveillance of employees is not a new phenomenon, electronic surveillance allows employers to monitor workers with unprecedented efficiency. In his book The Naked Employee, Frederick Lane describes offline ways in which employers have been permitted to intrude on employees' privacy for decades, such as drug testing, background checks, psychological exams, lie detector tests, and in-store video surveillance. The difference, Lane argues, between these old methods of data gathering and electronic surveillance involves quantity:

Technology makes it possible for employers to gather enormous amounts of data about employees, often far beyond what is necessary to satisfy safety or productivity concerns. And the trends that drive technology--faster, smaller, cheaper--make it possible for larger and larger numbers of employers to gather ever-greater amounts of personal data. (3-4)

Title centered, with space on both sides

1" margins on all sides

Text double-spaced

First line of each paragraph indented

Long quotation indented in MLA style

FIGURE V3-8 Effective use of white space in a student paper
The formatting required in MLA style provides ample white space that enhances readability and allows for written comments.
(*Source:* Diana Hacker, *A Writer's Reference*, 6th edition)

Effective use of space is also important in visual presentations, such as transparencies or PowerPoint slides. Providing ample space and limiting the text on each slide helps readers absorb your main points (see Figures V3–9 and V3–10). Text on your slides is meant only to summarize major issues and themes, not to provide details; you can flesh out your main points during your talk.

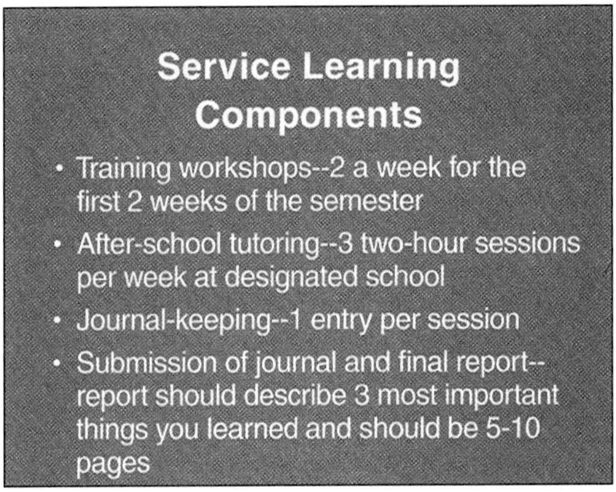

Service Learning Components

- Training workshops--2 a week for the first 2 weeks of the semester
- After-school tutoring--3 two-hour sessions per week at designated school
- Journal-keeping--1 entry per session
- Submission of journal and final report-- report should describe 3 most important things you learned and should be 5-10 pages

FIGURE V3-9 **Ineffective use of white space**
This presentation slide has too much text and too little white space. It is hard to read and potentially distracting for the audience.

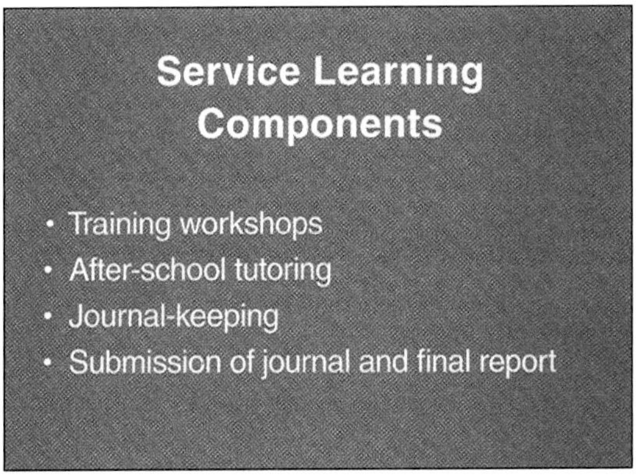

Service Learning Components

- Training workshops
- After-school tutoring
- Journal-keeping
- Submission of journal and final report

FIGURE V3-10 **Effective use of white space**
This presentation slide lists only the major points and has more white space. It is easier to read and grasp.

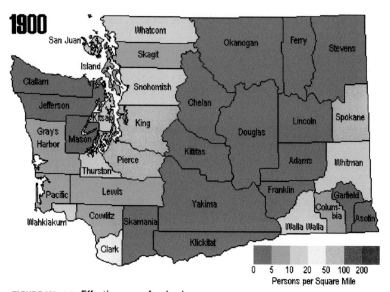

FIGURE V3-11 Effective use of color in a map
Varying shades and colors show population density. (*Source:* State of Washington)

Colorful images draw the eye and link to featured exhibitions and events on the home page.

Green headers are used for links to one type of resource, blue for another.

Additional color images illustrate links.

FIGURE 3-12 Effective use of color on a Web page (*Source:* Smithsonian Institution)

V3-e Use color to promote understanding and focus your readers' attention.

Word processing software and other programs make it easy to include color graphics, photographs, and other images in documents. Use color only for a specific purpose, such as highlighting key information or focusing attention on important elements (see Figure V3–11).

On a Web page, you can use color to highlight headings and other key information as well as attract and keep readers' attention (see Figure V3–12). Avoid using too many different colors because they can distract readers and defeat the purpose of helping them find important information. Also, choose colors carefully. For example, although yellow is an attention-getting color, words written in yellow on a white background are difficult to read.

V4

Using visuals to support text

Your visuals and text should work together to achieve your purpose and meet your readers' needs. Visuals can support your text by emphasizing information, conveying information that is difficult to explain with words, consolidating information, and capturing your readers' attention. Visuals should support, not overshadow, the content of your document. Too many visuals without explanations might make your document difficult to understand. Try to strike a balance between the number and size of your visuals and the related text.

V4-a Decide what type of visual to use.

When deciding what type of visual to use, consider the ways in which different types of visuals can support your purpose and help your readers (see "visuals" in your handbook). To discuss a conflict among countries, supply a map. To illustrate an autobiographical essay, scan an image of yourself as a baby or at some important moment in your life. To explain a wastewater treatment process or activities at an archaeological dig, include a diagram or an illustration (see Figure V4–1).

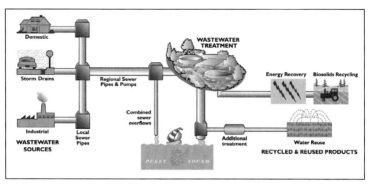

FIGURE V4–1 **Diagram of wastewater treatment process**
Diagrams can show how components work together. Usually the major components
are labeled, as in this diagram. (*Source:* King County, Washington, Department of Natural
Resources Wastewater Treatment Division)

Your topic and the kind of information you wish to convey will
also help you decide what types of visuals to use. For example, in a
college essay on the benefits of following a vegetarian diet, you
might use a table to compare resources needed to produce different
food types, a line graph to show a trend in meat consumption, a
photograph to show vegetarian food options, a pie chart for the percentage of vegetarian meals eaten by a population, and a diagram
for diet guidelines (see Figure V4–2).

V4-b Place and label your visual.

Placing the visual close to the related discussion will make your
document easier to follow. Readers can become distracted if they
must flip to a different page or an appendix to see a visual. Label
your visual (Figure 1, Table 3.4, and so on), number it, and include
a descriptive title (see Figure V4–3). Because tables and figures are
numbered separately, you can have a Table 1 and a Figure 1 in the
same document. If your document includes many figures and tables,
consider putting a list of visuals at the beginning of your document
so that your readers can easily find them.

V4-c Introduce and explain your visual.

Because you are including visuals to support ideas in your text,
your readers will make better sense of the visuals if you provide

TABLE

FIGURE V4–2 **Types of visuals that could support a paper on the benefits of following a vegetarian diet** (*Sources:* [top to bottom] Humane Society of the United States, US Department of Agriculture, City of Santa Monica, Humane Society of the United States, US Department of Agriculture)

Resources	To Produce One Pound of Processed Soy Protein	To Produce One Pound of Processed Animal Protein
Land Needed	1	6 to 17
Water Needed	1	4.4 to 26
Fossil Fuel Needed	1	6 to 20

LINE GRAPH

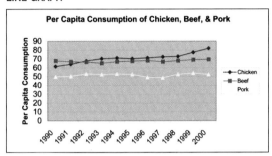

PIE CHART

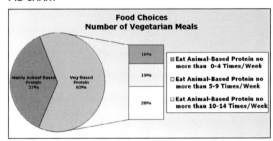

PHOTOGRAPH

DIAGRAM

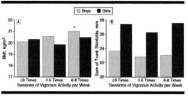

FIGURE V4–3 A text paragraph and related visuals

Visuals are placed near the discussion of them in the text. Labels for each type of visual should be placed consistently throughout a document. Here the table label is positioned above the table, the figure label below the figure. (*Source:* American Medical Association)

context for them. You should refer to a visual by number and explain the point that it helps you make (see Figure V4–3). For complicated visuals or for visual types with which your readers might not be familiar (such as a schematic diagram or a bathymetric chart), explain how to interpret the visual.

V4-d Credit your sources.

If you include a visual from another source, credit that source in your document (see "avoiding plagiarism" in your handbook). Credit the source of any data that you use in a visual, even if you create the visual yourself. You must also credit your source if you significantly revise a visual or use only portions of a visual from another source (see Figure V4-4). If you include copyrighted visuals in a document you intend to publish (in print or on the Web), you must credit your source and obtain written permission from the copyright holder.

> Source: Modified from Ray et al. 1997. Reproduced from J Bone Miner Res 1997: Jan; 12(1): 24–35 with permission of the American Society for Bone and Mineral Research.

FIGURE V4-4 **Visual adapted from another visual**
This source line, which appears at the bottom of a table in a technical journal, indicates that the author adapted ("modified") the table from another source. The author credits the source and indicates that the copyright holder provided permission to use the visual. (*Source:* US Department of Health and Human Services)

Document design checklist

Document design

- Does your document design help to achieve your purpose?
- Does your document design meet your readers' needs and expectations?
- Does your document design help readers quickly find the information they seek?
- Does your document design help to emphasize your key points and make important information stand out?

Organization

- Do your headings guide your readers and reveal a clear organization?
- Have you repeated elements such as running headers or footers to help readers understand where they are in your document?

Visuals

- Do your visuals convey useful information and support your text?
- Have you used the most effective types of visuals for your purpose?

Document design checklist (continued)

- Have you introduced and explained each of your visuals in the text of your document?
- Have you credited the source of each visual? Have you secured any permission needed to use copyrighted material?

Design elements

- Have you used appropriate fonts in your document? Do you use bold-face and italic styles sparingly and only for emphasis?
- Have you used displayed lists when appropriate to emphasize information or explain a sequence?
- Does the white space in your document frame important information?
- Have you used color effectively to highlight or organize information?

EXERCISE V1 Designing documents

1. Open a paragraph or two from a recent paper in your word processing software. Use the font list in the word processor to see how your sentences look in different fonts. Test sizes as well as bold and italic styles. Choose four very different fonts and discuss in a short paper the legibility of each font as well as the situations in which each font would be appropriate.
2. Look at a bulletin board, magazine shelf, or other location where many examples of printed material are displayed. Identify several different uses of fonts to establish a particular tone. Select one example that you find particularly effective, and briefly explain in a paper how the font helps to convey the desired tone to readers. If possible, include a copy of the example with your paper.
3. Locate an online or print copy of a research paper or report. Skim the report to answer the following questions.

   a. What is the purpose of the report?

   b. Who are the intended readers? How can you tell?

   c. In what ways does the writer use document design strategies to address readers' needs?

   d. How does the writer use document design strategies to make his or her point?

   e. What design revisions would you recommend to the writer? How might these changes improve the reading experience of the intended readers?

   Write a brief essay presenting your findings.

4. Locate an online or a print copy of a paper or report that uses several visuals. Skim the paper or report to answer the following questions.

   a. What is the purpose of the report?

   b. Who are the intended readers?

   c. How effectively do the types of visuals suit the readers and the purpose of the report?

   d. In what ways does the writer use visuals to convey information?

   e. How effectively does the writer place, label, size, and align the visuals?

   f. How effectively does the writer introduce and explain the visuals?

   g. How does the writer credit the source of each visual?

   Write a brief essay presenting your findings.

5. **For group work.** Collect several different academic and business documents that you are currently reading or might read. Examine each document carefully, considering which aspects of the design seem effective or ineffective in achieving the writer's purpose and meeting the needs of the readers. When you've finished your analysis, share your findings with the rest of the class.

6. **For group work.** Examine several different academic and business documents. For each document, consider what other design choices might have made the document more effective. When you've finished your analysis, share your findings with the rest of the class.

UNDERSTANDING VISUALS

Whether a visual is part of a document or stands alone, it was most likely created for a specific purpose. Some visuals are created to capture and maintain your attention. Others try to shape your buying habits and opinions. A billboard, for example, might try to persuade you to buy a certain brand of laundry detergent or convince you to vote for a particular political candidate.

Most of the visuals you encounter in academic and business documents are created to communicate information. While researching a paper on Internet addiction, you might consult a table showing the relationship between hours spent on the Internet and Internet addiction test scores, a pie chart showing the most common types of Internet addiction, and a bar graph comparing Internet addiction behaviors of men and women. In business, you might consult a table consolidating a decade of water quality test data, an organizational chart showing your immediate supervisor, or a line graph emphasizing rising utility costs. In an art or writing course, you might analyze and interpret a photograph or a painting. Making sense of these visuals is a critical first step in understanding and using the information they communicate.

Charts, tables, graphs, photographs, and advertisements are not the only visuals you will need to understand in a college class and the business world. You will also encounter cartoons, drawings, maps, and logos from a variety of sources with a variety of purposes. The skills you develop for understanding visuals will help you become a more critical reader of visuals and of documents with supporting visuals. Developing visual literacy skills will also help you become better at identifying opportunities to use visuals to communicate messages and choosing the best types of visuals to achieve your purpose and meet your readers' needs.

V5

Four steps to understanding a visual

Begin a visual analysis by conducting a close reading of the visual. Like a critical reading of a written text, understanding a visual involves careful, in-depth examination. Your close reading should follow these four steps:

1. Identify the context for the visual. What is the source of the visual and who created it? What is its purpose? What readers does it address?
2. Identify the type of visual. Is the visual a table, a drawing, a photograph, a graph, an advertisement? What is its general purpose? Does the visual have text, numbers, or images?
3. Study the parts of the visual. What are the major elements of the visual? How are they designed and arranged? What choices did the creator of the visual make when presenting the parts of the visual?
4. Determine the main idea. What do the numbers, text, and images mean? What is the main point of the visual?

You might discover that other people respond differently to some visuals than you do. Each person's background and experiences influence how he or she interprets the meaning of a visual. Images such as those used in advertisements and photographs often communicate different meanings to different readers. Likewise, readers might arrive at different conclusions while looking at the same numbers in a table. The steps explained in this section will help you record your observations and interpretations in an organized manner and help you support your conclusions with evidence from the visual.

V6

Step 1: Identifying the visual's context

Begin your close reading of a visual by examining its context. If the visual is part of a document, step back from the visual and consider the document as a whole. Find out who wrote the document and why. The intended readers of the document as well as its purpose will provide you with clues to help you understand its visuals. If the visual stands alone, consider where it appears — in an art exhibit, an ad campaign, a billboard, and so on. Find out the theme or purpose of its location as well as its sponsors. Once you have a good idea of the environment in which the visual exists, look more closely at the visual and its role.

V6-a Determine the source.

Locate the source of the visual or, if appropriate, the source of the elements used to create it. If a designer produces his or her own visuals and uses his or her own data, the visual will not have a source listed. But if a visual is not original, it will usually have a source crediting the person or organization that created it (see Figure V6–1). The source is usually located at the bottom of the visual. Sometimes the source is listed in the acknowledgments or in the endnotes in a document. If the visual includes text, numbers, or images from other sources, these elements will also be credited.

Once you determine the source of the visual, evaluate whether the visual contains accurate, current, and unbiased information (see "evaluating sources" in your handbook). Consider whether the source is credible. A map produced by the US Coast Guard indicating shipping lanes in a harbor is likely to be accurate, for example. Next check the date listed in the source. Data from the 1980s is not as useful as data from 2006 if you are writing about *current* trends in voter participation in local elections. Consider also whether the

© Fred Zwicky, 2004. Used with permission.
This photograph originally appeared in the *Peoria Journal Star.*

FIGURE 6-1 Source statement
A source statement indicates who created the visual or who owns the rights to it, when it was created, and sometimes where it first appeared. (*Source:* Fred Zwicky, 2004)

source has a stake in the topic. The National Milk Producers Federation might report different data on the value of daily milk consumption than the American Dietetic Association would give.

V6-b Identify the purpose and audience.

Consider why the writer included the visual in the document; if the visual stands alone, consider why the designer or artist created the visual. The purpose of a visual will often suggest what you should pay most attention to. If a visual is included to capture or maintain your attention, you don't need to spend much time looking for a deeper message. If a visual is used to capture the excitement of a rodeo event, you can look more closely at the facial expressions of the crowd and competitors (see Figure V6–2). If a visual is used to show the stages of a process, you can look more closely at the individual stages and how they are related (see Figure V6–3). If a

FIGURE V6-2 Photograph capturing emotion and action

The purpose of this photo is to capture the emotion and action in a rodeo. The crowd's reaction in the background draws viewers' eyes as much as the main action does. (*Source:* Professional Bull Riders, Inc.)

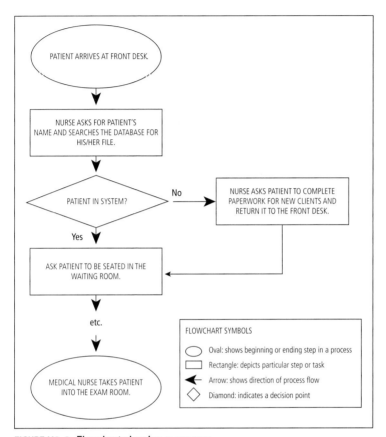

FIGURE V6-3 **Flowchart showing a process**
A flowchart invites close attention to every step of a process or a decision.
(*Source:* New York State Department of Health AIDS Institute)

visual is used to sell a product, you can note how text and images work together to persuade readers (see Figure V6–4).

Along with considering the purpose, determine the intended audience for the visual. The readers for a visual are frequently the same as the readers for the document or exhibit in which the visual appears. Examining the level of detail and choice of images contained in the visual will help you identify the readers for the visual (see Figure V6–5). Once you determine the intended audience, you can evaluate how effectively the visual meets its readers' needs and expectations (see V1-b).

FIGURE V6–4 Advertisement combining text and image
Advertisements feature text and images in combination to convince
consumers of the product's benefits. (*Source:* American Honda Motor Co., Inc.)

V7

Step 2: Identifying the type of visual

Learning to understand different types of visuals takes practice and
experience. Each type of visual has its own set of defined features and
conventions for displaying data.

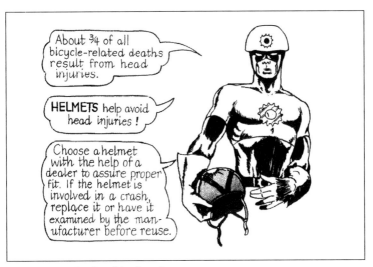

FIGURE V6–5 **Visual on bicycle safety**
The cartoon image and simple language suggest that this visual is intended for young readers. (*Source:* US Consumer Product Safety Commission)

Maps use symbols for geographic features and points of interest, such as a blue line to represent a stream or a small tent to represent a campground. Charts show lines or bars in relation to horizontal and vertical scales (see Figure V7–1). Tables display numbers and words in columns and rows. Advertisements tell a story with pictures and words. Photographs often show key elements — the elements the photographer wants viewers to see right away — in the upper left quadrant of the photo (see Figure V7–2). Once you identify the parts of a visual, you can begin to consider how the parts work together to communicate a message.

You read visuals differently depending on their type. When people read a table, they usually start at the top left and read across the column heads and then down the columns from left to right. When people read a line graph, they usually start at the left and follow the line as it moves across the graph. Pie charts require readers to consider the relation of each pie slice to the other slices and to the whole. Most Americans and Europeans view a picture from left to right and top to bottom, creating a Z pattern with their eye movements (see Figure V7–3). The features of the visual — text, numbers, images, and so on — provide clues as to the type of visual and, consequently, how it should be read or interpreted.

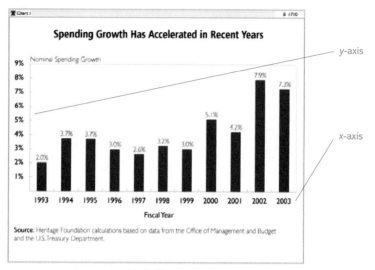

FIGURE V7–1 Bar graph with horizontal and vertical scales

The two axes of a bar graph show the relationship between two types of numerical data. In this case, the vertical scale, or *y*-axis, represents growth rate as a percentage; the horizontal scale, or *x*-axis, represents time in fiscal years. (*Source:* The Heritage Foundation)

FIGURE V7–2 Photograph divided into quadrants

Key elements of the photo appear in the upper left quadrant. The focus is on the children's reaction to what they are reading.
(*Source:* Kodak Picture of the Day, October 22, 2000)

FIGURE V7–3 **Z pattern for reading images**
The eye moves from left to right, top to bottom, in a *Z* pattern when viewing a photograph. (*Source:* Kodak Picture of the Day, October 22, 2000)

V7-a Look for text.

Text in visuals usually appears in titles, legends, and labels. Tables use text in column and row heads to label data (see Figure V7–4). Diagrams use text to label steps, parts, or concepts (see Figure V7–5). Advertisements use text to capture readers' attention, suggest a

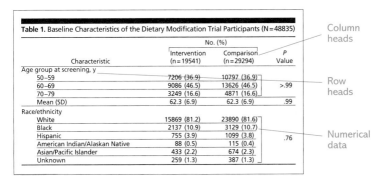

Table 1. Baseline Characteristics of the Dietary Modification Trial Participants (N = 48835)			
	No. (%)		
Characteristic	Intervention (n = 19541)	Comparison (n = 29294)	P Value
Age group at screening, y			
50–59	7206 (36.9)	10797 (36.9)	
60–69	9086 (46.5)	13626 (46.5)	>.99
70–79	3249 (16.6)	4871 (16.6)	
Mean (SD)	62.3 (6.9)	62.3 (6.9)	.99
Race/ethnicity			
White	15869 (81.2)	23890 (81.6)	
Black	2137 (10.9)	3129 (10.7)	
Hispanic	755 (3.9)	1099 (3.8)	.76
American Indian/Alaskan Native	88 (0.5)	115 (0.4)	
Asian/Pacific Islander	433 (2.2)	674 (2.3)	
Unknown	259 (1.3)	387 (1.3)	

Column heads

Row heads

Numerical data

FIGURE V7–4 **Text within a table**
Tables use text in column heads and row heads to label, organize, and describe numerical data. (*Source:* American Medical Association)

mood, or describe a product (see Figure V7–6). Sometimes a visual uses a special set of symbols as shorthand to communicate information concisely (see Figure V7–7).

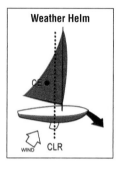

FIGURE V7-5 Text in a diagram
Labels identify concepts in a basic sailing text. The labels are defined in the text that accompanies the diagram: CE for center of effort and CLR for center of lateral resistance. (*Source:* American Sailing Association)

FIGURE V7-6 **Text in an advertisement**
The company's slogan *Go. Do. Be.* suggests travel, action sports, and determination. (*Source:* Teva, 2006)

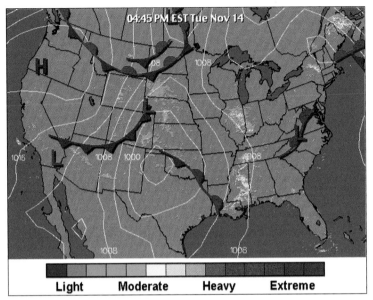

FIGURE V7-7 Symbols in a weather map
Colored letters show high (H) and low (L) pressure points, and symbols indicate warm, cold, and stationary fronts. The color scale at the bottom indicates rainfall amounts. (*Source:* The Weather Underground)

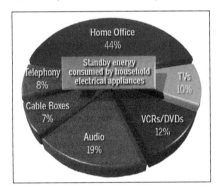

FIGURE V7-8 Pie chart
A pie chart shows each part as a percentage of the whole. This pie chart represents electrical consumption for different appliances when they are switched off (on standby) as a percentage of total electrical standby use. (*Source: Discover* magazine)

V7-b Look for numbers.

Numbers in visuals communicate quantities, scales, money, time, ratios, rankings, and percentages. Tables, charts, and graphs are the most common visuals containing numbers. Tables arrange numbers in columns and rows (see Figure V7–4). Pie charts use percentages to show the relative sizes of the parts of a whole (see Figure V7–8). Line and bar graphs use numbers to indicate values and trends (see Figure V7–9).

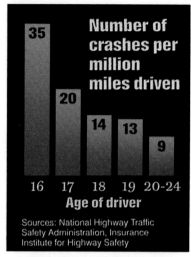

FIGURE V7–9 Bar graph

A bar graph can show comparisons at a glance, in this case how the number of crashes decreases as the age of the driver increases. (*Source: US News & World Report*)

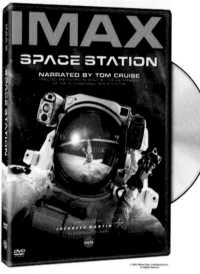

FIGURE V7–10 Advertisement with a dominant image and brief text

The dominant image of an astronaut with the reflection of the space station in the visor suggests the topic of the movie. The minimal text identifies merely the type of movie (IMAX), the name of the movie, the narrator, and the sponsors. (*Source:* Warner Bros. Entertainment Inc.)

V7-c Look for images.

Images dominate some visuals. For example, some advertisements are exclusively composed of images such as pictures, drawings, and cartoons. Other advertisements are predominantly made of images

how much is a serving? a 21st-century guide

STANDARD FOOD SERVING guidelines—like figuring a serving of meat for a cassette tape—are so last century. Since debit cards and personal digital assistants (PDAS) have replaced checkbooks and date books in your purse, here's a modern way to spot serving sizes:

FOOD ITEM	MODERN EQUIVALENT
a medium potato	the mini (6 oz.) soda can
3 ounces of meat	floppy disk
one scoop of ice cream	a round iMac mouse
3 ounces of grilled fish	PDA
1 ounce of cheese	pager
1 tablespoon of olive oil (or other cooking oil)	an individual eye-shadow compact
a serving of pretzels or other snack food	a coffee mug's full

FIGURE V7-11 **Images added to a text-based visual**
The text and the table could stand on their own, but the images add visual interest. (*Source: Health* magazine)

with only a small amount of text (see Figure V7–10). Visuals such as maps, diagrams, and photographs rely heavily on images to communicate information. In addition, some visuals convey their information primarily in words, and images are added just to capture readers' attention (see Figure V7–11).

V8

Step 3: Studying the parts of the visual

Once you have identified the type of visual and its features, you are ready to focus on each element of the visual — observing and considering each objectively rather than trying to draw any conclusions at this point.

V8-a Read any text and numbers.

Start by reading the title, labels, and legend, if the visual has those elements. A well-written title will tell you the topic of the visual. Labels identify parts of a visual, units of measurement, and key features. Legends identify elements not labeled elsewhere on the visual (see Figure V8–1). In a document, read passages that refer to or comment on the visual (see Figure V8–2).

Determine the purpose of any numbers. In academic and business documents, numbers often quantify variables. Variables represent what was measured, such as height, interest rates, distance, number of people, degrees Fahrenheit, and so on (see Figure V8–3). In advertisements, numbers might represent prices, addresses, telephone numbers, or product names.

V8-b Study any images.

Examine the types, colors, sizes, and positions of the images included in the visual. Look closely at any figures (humans or even animals) in the visual. Consider facial expression, pose, hairstyle and color, age, sex, ethnicity, possible education, suggested occupation, apparent relationship to one another, and so on.

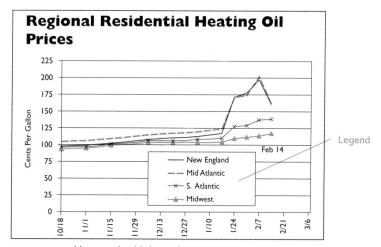

FIGURE V8-1 **Line graph with legend**
The legend tells readers what each type of line represents. (*Source:* Energy Information Administration/State Energy Office Data)

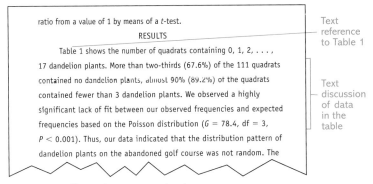

FIGURE V8-2 **Text reference to a visual**
(*Source:* Tom Jehn and Jane Rosenzweig, *Writing in the Disciplines: Advice and Models*)

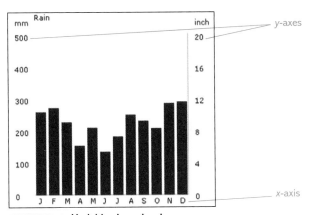

FIGURE V8-3 **Variables in a visual**
The graph shows two variables: time of year by
month (horizontal or *x*-axis) and rainfall in inches
and millimeters (vertical or *y*-axes). (*Source:* World66)

V8-c Examine how text, numbers, and images are designed and arranged.

Reflect on how the elements of the visual — text, numbers, images —
are organized and relate to one another (see Figure V8–4). Think about
the following questions.

- Is there one major element — object, person, number, background, text — in the visual that immediately attracts your
  attention? How and why does this element draw you into
  the visual?

FIGURE V8-4 Text and images in an advertisement
The combination of the silhouetted figure, posed to resemble a cross, and the snow-covered peaks and clouds in the background suggests a spiritual experience. Minimal text on the image presents the company name and slogan. The wordier text below the image connects a sense of adventure with the company's product, the parka at the lower left. (*Source:* Marmot)

- What are the major colors and shapes?
- How are elements arranged? Are some grouped closer to others? Does the distance between elements suggest something about their relationship?
- Does the visual appear balanced? Are elements grouped in one part of the visual, leaving another part empty?
- Does the visual appear organized or chaotic?

- Is one area of the visual darker or brighter than other areas?
- What does the design make you think of — does it bring to mind a particular emotion, historical period, or memory?

V8-d Consider choices made by the author.

When you look at a document, consider why the author might have chosen to include a visual or, if the visual stands alone, why the designer might have composed it in a particular way. Authors and designers can choose visuals for their appeal to readers, for the information they contain, or for the way they present information (see Figure V8–5). Beyond choosing the type of visual, they also choose which elements to include, which elements to emphasize, and how to display them (see Figures V8–6 and V8–7). Sometimes what is missing from a visual is as important as what is included. For example, you might notice the absence of people of color or people with disabilities in an advertisement for a school. The choices made by an author or a designer often provide clues as to the purpose and the message of the visual.

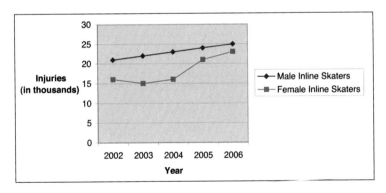

Year	Male Inline Skaters	Female Inline Skaters
2002	21,196	16,007
2003	22,051	15,202
2004	23,211	16,000
2005	23,998	21,212
2006	25,004	23,109

FIGURE V8–5 Information displayed in two types of visuals
These visuals present the same information in two different ways. The line graph allows readers to see quickly the trend in injuries. The table provides exact numbers for comparison.

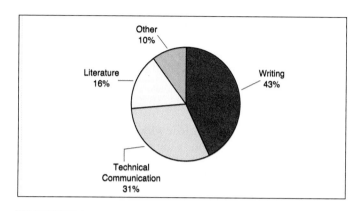

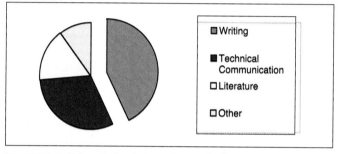

FIGURE V8-6 Using display features for emphasis

The top pie chart presents all the data numerically, with a percentage attached to each slice of the pie. The bottom chart, an *exploded* pie chart, emphasizes one slice and provides no numerical data. Readers make general conclusions based on the relative sizes of the slices and on the slice the author chose to pull out of the whole.

V9

Step 4: Determining the main idea

After examining the parts of a visual, you are ready to determine the main idea. For tables, charts, and graphs, you can describe what is being measured and compared. For visuals relying on images, you can determine the story, mood, or message. Your findings will help you understand the main point of the visual.

FIGURE V8-7 **Cropping for emphasis**
The wide-angle view (left) emphasizes the larger context. The cropped photo (right) focuses on the figure of the climber, without background distractions but also without the complete context.

V9-a Interpret text, numbers, and images.

Text often plays a supporting role in tables, charts, and graphs. Text identifies and describes numbers and images, allowing you to understand what they mean. Text is often used in more subjective ways in advertisements, where interpretation is more personal, revealing individual and cultural values. Frequently advertisements use wordplay to communicate their messages. Often such ads are lighthearted, but they sometimes have a more serious tone (see Figure V9–1). Consider whether text provides information, generates an emotional response, or does both. Text might repeat a sound or concept, signal a comparison (such as "new, improved"), carry sexual overtones, issue a challenge, or offer advice (see Figure V9–2).

Numbers help you make comparisons and notice trends. When interpreting numbers, identify what is being compared, look for general patterns, and note any exceptions to patterns. Next consider the direction and size of the comparisons, patterns, and exceptions (see Figure V9–3).

FIGURE V9–1 **Wordplay with a serious message**
This advertisement uses a play on words to pitch a serious message.
The word *tolerance* is scrambled on the chalkboard so that the letters
in the center read *learn*. The chalkboard, a typical feature of the
classroom, suggests that tolerance is a basic lesson to be learned.
(*Source: Design for Communication: Conceptual Graphic Design Basics*)

Consider what feeling or mood an image creates and how it
does so. Images of confetti and balloons suggest a festive mood. In
an advertisement for a city recycling program, an image of a polluted
river with cans lining its banks might cause some readers to react
with feelings of disgust or shame or motivate them to participate in
recycling.

FIGURE V9–2 **Volkswagen advertisement, about 1959**
The words *Think small* suggest that compactness is a quality to be desired
in a car and, by extension, in life. The message can be interpreted to mean
"scale down"—lead a less consumer-oriented lifestyle.

Images can also communicate attitudes held by groups of people
(see Figure V9–2). Symbols, such as product logos, are images or
words that can also communicate key messages that an author or a
company wants to impress on viewers. A US flag held by a little boy
who is watching a Fourth of July parade with his family might sym-
bolize for some readers family values and patriotism. Sometimes a

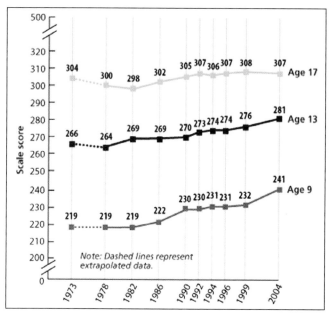

FIGURE V9-3 **Line graph showing trends**
The line graph demonstrates that while math scores for elementary and middle school students have shown dramatic improvement since the early 1970s, math scores for high school students have remained fairly steady. The visual suggests that learning in elementary and middle schools is not translating into higher achievement in high school. (*Source:* Achieve, Inc.)

product logo alone may be enough, as in the Hershey Company's holiday ads that include little more than a single Hershey's Kiss. The shape of the Kiss serves as a symbol for the company.

V9-b Analyze the main point.

The main point of a visual is not the same as a summary of its data or a description of its plot. When you summarize the data, you put into words what the visual shows. When you describe the plot, you explain the story that is told by an image. However, when you analyze the main point, you explain what the visual is about — what message it communicates.

A bar graph might show the average starting salaries for graduates with engineering degrees and English degrees, but the main point conveyed by the graph might be that entry-level engineers make 40 percent more money than entry-level high school English teachers. Likewise, the main point of a pie chart showing participation in an undergraduate internship program might be that the majority of college students complete at least one internship before they graduate.

An ad for a diamond ring might tell the story of a man surprising his wife with a ring on their twenty-fifth wedding anniversary, but the advertisement's main point might be that giving a diamond ring is a romantic way to celebrate the longevity of a marriage. Similarly, the main point of a sports drink ad might be that to maintain your high performance during an athletic event requires replenishing your energy. In Figure V9–4, you might argue that the photographer's message is that faith provides comfort in times of adversity, supporting your claim with references to details in the photo. Through a close reading of a visual, you can identify clues and details to support your interpretation of the main point and convince others of its merit.

FIGURE V9–4 **Analyzing a photograph**
This photograph can be analyzed in a number of ways, each analysis relying on details in the image, such as the woman's expression, her action, what she is holding, the debris in the background, the hymnal in the foreground, the telephone pole in the shape of a cross in the background, and so on.
(*Source:* Fred Zwicky, 2004)

Understanding visuals checklist

Step 1: Identify the context.

- Who created the visual or collected the information used in the visual? When was the visual created or the data collected?
- Why did the writer include the visual or the artist create the visual?
- Who are the intended readers or viewers?

Step 2: Identify the type of visual.

- What type of visual is this?
- What are the features of the visual?

Step 3: Study the parts of the visual.

- What does the text tell you about the visual?
- What do the numbers represent?
- What images are present?
- How are text, numbers, and images designed and arranged?
- What choices did the author or designer make when creating the visual?

Step 4: Determine what is being communicated.

- What comparisons, generalizations, or feelings do the text, numbers, and images communicate?
- What is the main point communicated by the visual?

EXERCISE V2 Understanding visuals

1. Pick a controversial topic and locate a document arguing one side of the controversy and another document representing the other side. Examine the visuals used in each document. What types of visuals does each document use? What are the sources of the visuals? What topics and points do the visuals support? In an essay, compare how each document uses visuals to achieve its purpose and meet its readers' needs.

2. Look through several journal articles and other documents from your discipline or field, collecting examples of different types of visuals. Choose an example of each type of visual you find and briefly describe its features and purpose in an essay. If possible, include copies of the visuals in your paper.

3. Visit a music store and find a CD cover whose design interests you. Make notes about design choices such as the most prominent element,

the use of color and imagery, and the use of typography. From the design, try to predict what kind of music is on the CD. If the store has CD-listening stations, listen to a track or two. Did the music match your expectations based on the CD design? If you were the CD designer, would you have made any different artistic choices? Write a brief essay discussing your observations. Attach a copy of the CD cover if possible.

4. Find a print ad that evokes a strong emotional response. Conduct a close reading of the ad, observing its parts and determining its meaning. Write an essay explaining the techniques the ad uses to evoke your emotional response. Include a copy of the ad with your essay. Consult others to determine whether they have the same response to the ad.

5. **For group work.** In a small group, find out nutritional data and prices for several menu items at two different restaurants. Use four different types of visuals to communicate this information: a table, a chart, a graph, and an advertisement. What choices did you have to make when creating each visual? In what ways are any of your visuals biased in favor of one of the restaurants? For each visual, discuss in class your choices, the purpose of the visual, and the intended audience.

6. **For group work.** In a small group, pick one or two images (for example, an advertisement; drawing; a photo from a magazine or image database; a CD, DVD, or videocassette cover). Ask each group member, in turn, to suggest possible interpretations of the meanings of the images. What different interpretations do group members suggest? How do you account for the differences in these interpretations? Share your findings with the class.

Acknowledgments *(continued from page V-ii)*

Figure V7–6: "Go. Do. Be." Teva advertisement. Reprinted with the permission of Deckers Outdoor Corporation.

Figure V7–7: Weather map. Courtesy Wunderground.com.

Figure V7–8: Excerpt from "Wasting Away on Standby" from *Discover* (December 2002). Copyright © 2002. Reprinted with the permission of *Discover*.

Figure V7–11: "How Much Is a Serving?" table. Copyright © 2002 by Hippocrates Partners. Reprinted with the permission of *Health*.

Figure V8–4: "Marmot for Life" advertisement. Reprinted with the permission of Marmot Mountain LLC.

Figure V9–2: "Think small." Vintage Volkswagen advertisement. Reprinted with the permission of Volkswagen of America.

Figure V9–3: Line graph. Reprinted with the permission of Achieve, Inc.

Figure V9–4: Photograph, 2004. Courtesy Fred Zwicky.

Index

NOTE: Page numbers in italics refer to pages with figures.